A+
books

King Cobras

Are Awesome!

by Megan Cooley Peterson

Consultant: Jackie Gai, DVM
Wildlife Vet

D1388250

Raintree is an imprint of Capstone Global Library Limited, a company incorporated in England and Wales having its registered office at 264 Banbury Road, Oxford, OX2 7DY – Registered company number: 6695582

www.raintree.co.uk
myorders@raintree.co.uk

Text © Capstone Global Library Limited 2016
The moral rights of the proprietor have been asserted.

Edited by Michelle Hasselius
Designed by Peggie Carley
Picture research by Tracy Cummins
Production by Morgan Walters
Printed and bound in China.

ISBN 978-1-474-70252-2 (hardcover)
19 18 17 16 15
10 9 8 7 6 5 4 3 2 1

ISBN 978-1-474-70259-1 (paperback)
20 19 18 17 16
10 9 8 7 6 5 4 3 2 1

British Library Cataloguing in Publication Data
A full catalogue record for this book is available from the British Library.

Acknowledgements
Agumbe Rainforest Research Station/King Cobra Telemetry Project/Dhiraj Bhaisare: 12, 13, 23, 24, 27; AP Images: Rolf Wilms/picture-alliance, 22; Capstone Press: 10; Getty Images: R. Andrew Odum, 26; National Geographic Creative: Malaysia Langkawi, 15; Nature Picture Library: Sandesh Kadur, 14, 25; Newscom: ANJEEV GUPTA/EPA, 29, BARBARA WALTON/EPA, 4, Dorling Kindersley Universal Images Group, 6, Ingram Publishing, 11; Shutterstock: A Periam Photography, 8, apiguide, 28, BENZINE, 9, CHAINFOTO24, Cover Right, Eric Isselee, Cover Back, Cover Top, 1, 20, 30, Heiko Kiera, Cover Bottom, 18, 32, Matthew Cole, 7, Miro Vrlik Photography, 16, PUMPZA, 17 Bottom, Rigamondis, Design Element, Sam DCruz, 21, Skynavin, 5, Wichy, 19; Thinkstock: takeo1775, 17 Top

We would like to thank Jackie Gai, DVM, for her invaluable help in the preparation of this book.

Contents

Stay away!

A hungry mongoose follows a slithering king cobra. The cobra rears up. It spreads a hood of skin around its neck. **Hiss!** The cobra warns the mongoose to stay away. The mongoose leaves to find an easier meal.

Like most snakes, king cobras will first try to flee from danger. They can also try to scare enemies. King cobras can lift their heads up to 1.8 metres (6 feet) off of the ground.

Bones in the cobra's neck spread out the skin. This makes the king cobra look bigger than it really is. A king cobra will attack if cornered.

The king cobra is the world's longest venomous snake. This reptile can grow up to 5.5 metres (18 feet) long. That's longer than some cars! But most king cobras grow to about 4 metres (13 feet). Adults weigh up to 9 kilograms (20 pounds).

Life in Asia

King cobras live in parts of India, southern China, and south-east Asia. They live on plains and in rainforests. King cobras climb trees, slither along the ground and swim in water.

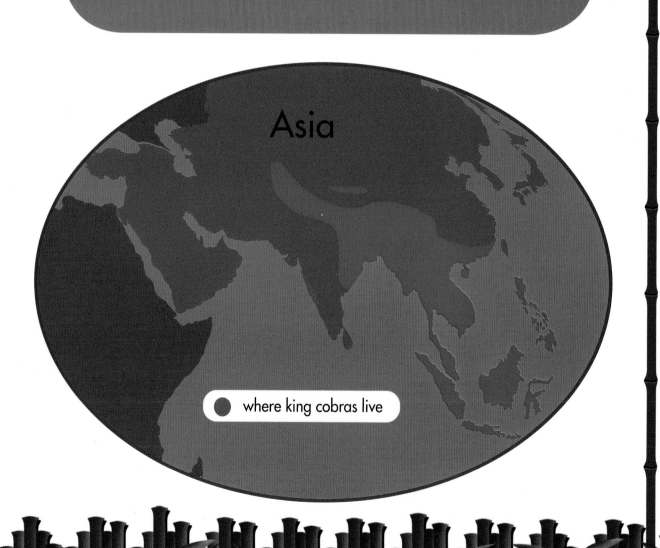

Asia

● where king cobras live

King cobras live alone. Because they are cold-blooded, cobras lie in the sun to warm up. To cool off, they look for shade.

Snack time! King cobras sneak along the forest floor and in the water. They mainly hunt other snakes. They also eat monitor lizards. A king cobra can strike an animal up to 1 metre (3 feet) away.

A king cobra bites its prey with two fangs in the front of its mouth. Hollow tubes in the fangs pump venom into its prey. One bite from a king cobra could kill an elephant!

Snakes swallow
their food whole. Their
bodies change food
into energy very slowly.
That's why king cobras
can go for weeks or
months between meals.

Snakes use their tongues to smell. First, the king cobra licks the ground. Its forked tongue picks up the scent. Then the snake puts its tongue into its Jacobson's organ. This is located on the roof of the snake's mouth. The Jacobson's organ helps the snake to smell its next meal.

A king cobra's large, round pupils see
well during the day. This snake can spot
prey up to 91 metres (300 feet) away.

King cobras can hear, but they don't have ear openings. The snake places its head on the ground to hear. Sounds travel through its head and into the inner ear.

The king cobra looks slimy. But smooth, dry scales cover its skin. Like your fingernails, a snake's scales are made of keratin. The king cobra's scales are yellow, brown, green or black. Large scales cover the tops of their heads. A clear scale covers each eye.

King cobras never stop growing. They shed their skin when they outgrow it. The cobra rubs its lips against a rock to break the skin. Then the snake wriggles out of its old skin.

the shed skin

Growing up

Female king cobras build nests out of dead leaves and twigs. No other snake builds nests. Females lay between 20 and 50 eggs in their nests. Females stay and guard their nests until their eggs hatch. A baby king cobra is called a hatchling.

hatchling

Hatchlings break out of their leathery eggs after about two months. They cut through their eggs using a sharp bump on their noses.

Hatchlings are about 46 centimetres (18 inches) long when they are born. Their scales are black with yellow or white stripes. Young king cobras live and hunt on their own. In the wild, king cobras live for about 20 years.

Saving king cobras

Hunters kill king cobras for their skins. They use cobras for food and to make medicine. When forests are cut down, king cobras lose their homes. Hunting and the loss of land mean that king cobras may soon become endangered.

People work to save king cobras. In
many places, it is illegal to kill king cobras.
Scientists also study cobras and set aside
land for these awesome Asian animals.

Glossary

cold-blooded having a body temperature that changes with the surrounding temperature

endangered in danger of dying out

fang long, pointed tooth

hatchling young animal that has just come out of its egg

hollow empty on the inside

keratin substance that makes up a person's hair, fingernails and toenails; a snake's scales are made of keratin

mongoose animal with a long tail and brown or black fur; mongooses are known for their ability to kill poisonous snakes

prey animal hunted by another animal for food

pupil dark centre of the eye that lets in light

reptile cold-blooded animal that breathes air and has a backbone; most reptiles have scales

scale small hard plate; scales cover the skins of reptiles and most fish

venom poisonous liquid produced by some animals

venomous having or producing venom

Books

Animals in Danger in Asia, Richard and Louise Spilsbury
(Raintree, 2013)

Introducing Asia (Introducing Continents), Anita Ganeri
(Raintree, 2014)

Remarkable Reptiles (Extreme Animals), Isabel Thomas
(Raintree, 2012)

Websites

http://animals.nationalgeographic.com/animals/reptiles/king-
cobra/
Learn all about king cobras.

www.bbc.co.uk/nature/life/King_Cobra
King cobras are the longest venomous snakes in the world. Find
out more fascinating facts about these reptiles.

http://gowild.wwf.org.uk/asia
Find out fun facts about king cobras, read stories and play games!

Comprehension questions

1. King cobras use venom to kill their prey. What is venom?

2. A king cobra doesn't have ear openings. How does the snake
   hear sounds?

3. Turn to page 28. What has happened in the photo? How can this
   impact king cobras?

Index